THE HUNTINGTON

LIBRARY   ART COLLECTIONS   BOTANICAL GARDENS

THE HUNTINGTON

LIBRARY   ART COLLECTIONS   BOTANICAL GARDENS

Text prepared by Peggy Park Bernal

HUNTINGTON LIBRARY
SAN MARINO, CALIFORNIA

THE HUNTINGTON
Library   Art Collections   Botanical Gardens
1151 Oxford Road San Marino, California 91108

GENERAL INFORMATION: 626.405.2141
MEMBERSHIP INFORMATION: 626.405.2290
BUSINESS OFFICES: 626.405.2100

www.huntington.org

FRONT COVER: The Huntington Library
BACK COVER: The Huntington Gallery with *Stag Hunt* by
Jacques Houzeau
BACK FLAP: Henry E. Huntington, ca. 1925
FRONTISPIECE: Frederic Edwin Church (1826–1900),
Chimborazo, 1864, oil on canvas (detail)

PHOTOGRAPHIC CREDITS: Kit Amorn, Lisa Blackburn,
Joe Clements, James Dice, Jerry Fredrick, Bruce Gelvin,
Don Milici, Clive Nichols, Don Normark, John Trager

Historical photographs from Huntington archives.
All photographs of the art and library collections by
John Sullivan and the Huntington Photo Services Department.

Second Edition 2003
Copyright © 2003, Henry E. Huntington Library and Art Gallery
This book, or parts thereof, may not be reproduced in any form
without permission
Printed in Hong Kong
ISBN: 0-87328-134-9 (paperback)
ISBN: 0-87328-143-8 (cloth)
Library of Congress Control Number 92-25873

CONTENTS

FROM THE PRESIDENT

WELCOME TO THE HUNTINGTON Library, Art Collections, and Botanical Gardens, an institution devoted to both public education and academic research in the humanities and sciences. Henry Huntington believed that an independent collection-based research library, free for use by scholars, would serve the community, the country, and the world in unique and important ways. After one hundred years, his vision has more than proven itself.

With one of the country's largest independent research libraries, the Huntington is a major center for humanistic scholarship and learning in the United States. Among the nearly eighteen hundred visiting scholars annually who conduct research using the extraordinary collection of rare books and manuscripts can be found Pulitzer Prize and National Book Award winners as well as Guggenheim and MacArthur Fellows. The founding of the United States, the Civil War, and the history of the American West are among the central research subjects at the Huntington. Few textbooks, whether for primary, secondary, or post-secondary schools, are untouched by the scholarly work that has been conducted here. In addition, the Huntington sponsors public lectures and academic conferences, which not only educate the broader populace but also stimulate additional research.

The gardens reinforce our educational mission. Mr. Huntington collected plants, just as he collected books and manuscripts. These plants—many of them rare or endangered—are incorporated into gardens that represent themed landscapes and cultural traditions. The Botanical Center, with its conservatory, children's garden, laboratories, and classrooms, enables us to strengthen scientific education in the region. The new Chinese garden will provide a remarkable opportunity to learn about the country's rich cultural heritage and landscape traditions.

The art collections also offer educational opportunities through public exhibitions, lectures, seminars, books, and classes. The Huntington's great collection of English masterpieces from

The Huntington Library

the eighteenth and nineteenth centuries, its broad collection of American art and artifacts, and its small but impressive collection of French furniture and sculpture, encourage learning for students of all ages. Major photography, drawing, and watercolor collections are used primarily by scholars. Changing exhibitions in the MaryLou and George Boone Gallery on individual artists, themes, or time periods enhance our educational offerings.

The Huntington works closely with regional universities and colleges, school districts, and teachers to strengthen their own educational activities. In addition, the institution's education department provides important programs for teachers to help them prepare the thousands of schoolchildren who visit the exhibitions and gardens each year. The Huntington's

public exhibitions on such historical themes as George Washington, Abraham Lincoln, and women's suffrage have been displayed in public libraries nationwide.

During your visit, you will be inspired by the beauty and allure of this place and its collections. Its size and complexity will impress you. But what you see is only a small part of what the Huntington is. I hope that you enjoy your visit and come back often. The Huntington is a place where all of us constantly learn.

Steven Koblik
President

HUNTINGTON HISTORY

THE SAN MARINO RANCH

SAN MARINO, CALIFORNIA IS KNOWN throughout the world as the location of the Huntington, with its famous library, its art gallery of masterpieces, and its unique botanical gardens. Yet before 1920, to most people "San Marino" meant the tiny republic between Forli and Pesaro in Italy. The name was planted in California in 1877, when James De Barth Shorb and his wife, Maria de Jesus Wilson, christened their ranch "San Marino," in memory of Shorb's boyhood home in Maryland. His grandfather, it is said, had so named his estate because its acreage was identical to that of the Italian republic.

Here, in the spring of 1892, the Shorbs entertained Henry E. Huntington, who was on a tour of Southern California in connection with railway business. The Shorb place, or rather its possibilities as a California home, stayed in his mind; he bought it ten years later.

THE HUNTINGTONS AT HOME

The home of Mr. and Mrs. Huntington, now the Art Gallery, was designed by Los Angeles architects Myron Hunt and Elmer Grey and built during the years 1909 to 1911. This handsome, spacious residence overlooking the San Gabriel Valley was first occupied by the Huntingtons in 1914. Its general style is Beaux Arts, adapted to the California climate and landscape.

The structure was very much as we know it today, except for the Main Gallery, which replaced a service wing. The rooms on the ground floor functioned as their names suggest, and the art objects found inside them formed an integral part of the living environment: meals were served in the dining room, cards

The Huntington residence, ca. 1920

The loggia of the Huntington residence in the 1920s

were played in one of the drawing rooms, and Mr. Huntington read in the library room amid the Louis XV furniture, with the Boucher tapestries on the walls around him.

The second floor was used for bedrooms: Mr. Huntington occupied the room located on the southeast corner in which conversation-piece portraits now hang, while Mrs. Huntington had an adjacent suite. The two secretaries, Mrs. Huntington's companion, and Mr. Huntington's valet had rooms on the second floor, and there was also space for guests. Frequent visitors included Sir Joseph Duveen (the Huntington's principal source for art objects), Dr. A. S. W. Rosenbach (the principal source for manuscripts and rare books in Mr. Huntington's later years), and Homer L. Ferguson, the president of the Newport News Shipbuilding and Dry Dock Company, a Huntington enterprise.

The Huntingtons' life in San Marino was relatively simple. The estate offered a number of diversions that everyone could enjoy, including the aviaries full of tropical birds and the

*Collis P. Huntington (left), newspaper boy, and Collis's nephew
Henry E. Huntington (right) in San Francisco, ca. 1892*

croquet lawn on the North Vista. There was a billiards room, a bowling alley, a pitch-and-putt golf course, and plenty of gardens for walking. A moderate amount of entertaining took place, particularly of family members. There were touches of elegance: only orange tree wood was used in the fireplaces, one dressed for dinner, and there were four footmen in attendance, even when the Huntingtons dined alone. Cards were played afterwards—bridge, if the group was sufficient; otherwise, hearts. To the west, the Huntingtons' neighbor was George Patton, father of the World War II general. It is said that the small canyon between the two properties was used as the stake in the card games played by the two friends, and that this piece of land changed hands as often as did their luck at cards.

HENRY EDWARDS HUNTINGTON: EARLY YEARS

Henry Edwards Huntington was born in 1850 in Oneonta, New York. At the age of twenty, he moved to New York City, intent on making his own way. A year later he joined the railroad enterprises of his uncle Collis P. Huntington. Their association lasted thirty years, up until Collis's death in 1900.

Both men were railroad executives at the time of the westward expansion. In 1892, H. E. Huntington moved to San Francisco to share with his uncle the management of the Southern Pacific Company, a holding company for the Southern Pacific and Central Pacific railroads. In 1902, H. E. Huntington withdrew from the management of the Southern Pacific, moved to Los Angeles, and bought the San Marino Ranch. His family remained in San Francisco, and his first marriage ended in divorce a few years later.

MR. HUNTINGTON IN LOS ANGELES

Mr. Huntington had great faith in the potential of Southern California to become a major commercial and cultural center. He began immediately to put his plans into effect to develop the area. He organized the Los Angeles interurban railway system, popularly known as the Red Cars, which provided quick, efficient, and inexpensive transportation throughout the greater Los Angeles area. He acquired large tracts of land for urban and suburban development and built the electric power and distribution systems that were necessary to support future growth.

In 1910, at the age of sixty, Mr. Huntington sold much of his interest in his urban railway system and began to devote most of his attention to books—his lifelong love—and to the growing collection that would one day form the nucleus of one of the greatest research libraries in the world.

Mr. Huntington's ambition was to build a preeminent research library that would concentrate on British and American history and literature. He bought manuscripts and rare books at a furious rate, frequently purchasing entire libraries, often at extremely high prices. He created a major collection in a few short years.

At the beginning, the books were kept in New York. As soon as the San Marino library building was completed in 1921, railroad cars full of books began to arrive in Southern California, where they were to be permanently housed.

As his book collections grew, Mr. Huntington also developed an interest in art, which he started collecting in 1907. He chose to specialize in British portraits of the eighteenth century. There can be little doubt that it was Arabella, the widow of Collis Huntington, who urged him to enlarge his collecting activities to include art as well as books. She was one of the wealthiest women in America and, especially after Collis's death in 1900, one of the most important collectors of her generation.

Henry Edwards and Arabella Huntington were married in 1913 when they were both in their early sixties, and they collected art together until Arabella died in 1924. Until his own death three years later, Mr. Huntington continued to add to the art collection as a memorial to his wife.

Mr. Huntington laid careful plans for the use of his collections. In 1919 he founded a research institution to serve scholars. The deed of trust establishing guidelines for the Huntington institution allowed for growth and flexibility to meet changing conditions. The Huntington Library, Art Collections, and Botanical Gardens is the contemporary embodiment of that founding indenture.

THE MAUSOLEUM

The mausoleum of Henry Edwards and Arabella Huntington is, perhaps, the most beautiful building on the grounds. Constructed of Colorado Yule marble, the mausoleum is located about a third of a mile northwest of the entrance pavilion, on a high point of the property overlooking the gardens. It was a favorite location on the grounds for the Huntingtons and, in fact, the place chosen by Mrs. Huntington for her burial site.

Mr. Huntington selected John Russell Pope (1874–1937), one of America's most distinguished architects, to design the mausoleum in the form of a Greek temple. Pope used a classic circular peristyle (or double colonnade) "because it presented a perfect front from every angle, and furthermore it was a combination of two perfect forms, the circle and sphere."

TOP LEFT: *Arabella Huntington, ca. 1910*
TOP RIGHT: *Henry E. Huntington, ca. 1925*
ABOVE: *The Huntington Mausoleum*

Pope later employed the same design in the construction of the Jefferson Memorial in Washington, D.C.

The Huntington memorial may be appreciated both as a graceful ornament to the gardens and as a solemn sepulcher. Four panels sculpted by John Gregory (1879–1958) are mounted on masonry piers that alternate with the columns of the inner peristyle. The panels represent the four seasons and are inscribed with verses to represent the four stages of life.

THE RESEARCH LIBRARY

MR. HUNTINGTON WAS interested in book collecting nearly all of his life, even retaining some books from his childhood. As a young man, he formed two libraries, selling the first so that he could buy out a partner in one of his early railroad businesses. By the age of sixty, he had accumulated enough wealth to retire and turn all of his attention to collecting books and manuscripts, primarily in British and American history and literature.

From 1910 until his death in 1927, Mr. Huntington acquired more than 200 entire libraries to form the core collections of the Library's research resources today. Notable among these libraries was the Elihu Dwight Church collection, which included the original manuscript of Benjamin Franklin's autobiography, twelve folios and thirty-seven quartos of Shakespeare, and rare first editions of Edmund Spenser and John Milton. From the sale of Robert Hoe's library, Mr. Huntington was able to purchase a copy of the Gutenberg Bible, one of eleven copies printed on vellum of a total of forty-eight copies known to have survived from the mid-fifteenth century.

Two examples of English libraries that Mr. Huntington acquired are the Kemble-Devonshire collection, noted for its plays and for twenty-five fifteenth-century books printed by William Caxton, England's first printer, as well as the Bridgewater Library of Lord Ellesmere, perhaps the greatest British family library dating from the sixteenth century, containing 4,400 early printed books and nearly 12,000 manuscripts, including the Ellesmere Chaucer, the most celebrated manuscript of the *Canterbury Tales*.

In 1920, Mr. Huntington moved his collections from New York City to the newly completed library building designed by Myron Hunt, and also moved his library staff and their families to California. The Library opened its doors to scholars in 1924 and ever since has steadily fulfilled the research and education mission intended by Mr. Huntington. The 1925 revision to the deed of trust states that the object of the institution is "the advancement of learning [in] the arts and sciences…to render

the books, manuscripts, and other contents available…to scholars and other persons engaged in research or creative work in history, literature, art, science, and kindred subjects,…and to prosecute and encourage study and research in original sources."

Today the library contains more than three times as many items as it did when Mr. Huntington created it. Nearly eighteen hundred post-doctoral scholars use the collections annually, attracted not only by the depth of the collections but also by what one scholar has called "perhaps the most wonderful research environment in the world." The Library shares these resources with the public through exhibitions and school and public programs created to advance the research and education mission of the Huntington.

MEDIEVAL MANUSCRIPTS

The Library's records related to the study of medieval England are unequaled in the United States. The collection contains more than four hundred manuscripts and several thousand English documents of great historical, literary, and religious interest.

Before the development of printing in the fifteenth century, all books and documents were written by hand. The earliest manuscript volume in the Library is the handsome Gundulf Bible, which dates from the first decades after the Norman Conquest of England in 1066 and was owned by the powerful Bishop Gundulf of Rochester.

To add beauty to their manuscripts, medieval scribes and artists decorated them with miniature paintings, embellished the capital letters with gold leaf and brilliant colors, and wove detailed floral borders around the text. One of the finest illuminated manuscripts, and the most important medieval book in the Huntington collections, is the Ellesmere manuscript of Geoffrey Chaucer's *Canterbury Tales* (ca. 1400–1410). Written on vellum, the manuscript is elaborately decorated with portraits of the twenty-three pilgrims of Chaucer's tales, including a likeness of the author himself. Its fame rests not only on its handsome presentation—it is one of the best-preserved English literary manuscripts in existence—but also on the importance of its text. The Ellesmere manuscript is one of the earliest and most complete copies of Chaucer's original text, made within a decade of the poet's death.

The Ellesmere Chaucer is in excellent condition partly because it remained undisturbed in the library of Sir Thomas Egerton and his family from the early seventeenth century until Mr. Huntington purchased the collection in 1917. The handsome binding is not original but was made in 1995 based on a style that was common in the early fifteenth century.

The most influential English poem of the Middle Ages, next to Chaucer's *Canterbury Tales*, is William Langland's *Piers Plowman*, a visionary poem written in the last quarter of the fourteenth century that explores the religious and social issues of the time. The Huntington holds four early manuscripts of the poem, in textually important variant versions.

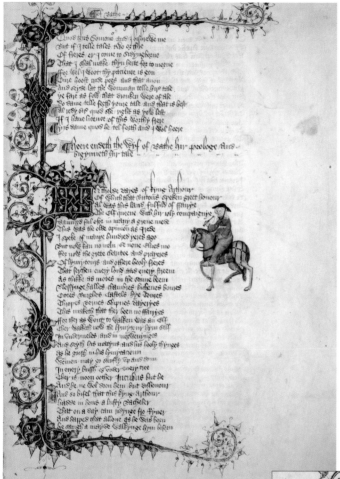

The beginning lines of Piers Plowman *in Middle English, from a manuscript written in the early fifteenth century*

The Ellesmere manuscript of the Canterbury Tales, *with a portrait of the* Wife of Bath

"In Principio," the opening words of the Book of Genesis from the manuscript Gundulf Bible, written in England in the eleventh century

Thought to be the earliest known portrait of Chaucer (ca. 1400–1410)

Books of Hours are among the most striking examples of illuminated manuscripts. These beautifully decorated books, used by wealthy men and women for their private religious devotions, contain prayers for the canonical hours into which the Catholic church divides each day. The leaves of such books were made of vellum, the text carefully written by professional scribes, the ornamental borders drawn by a specialist in decorations, and the miniature pictures (usually scenes from the life of the Virgin Mary) painted by a master artist.

The Library occasionally displays leaves from the manuscript Book of Hours illuminated between 1450 and 1475 by the famous artist Simon Marmion; it is one of the finest of the seventy-eight Books of Hours in the collection.

requiescant in pace. Amen. Ad cō
pletor:

on uer
te nos
deus sa
lutaris
noster:
et auer
te iram
tuam
a nob̄.

eus in adiutoriū meū intēde.
Dñe ad adiuuandū me festina.
Gloria patri et filio et spū sc̄o.
Sicut erat in principio et nunc
et semp et in secula sclōz a. Allā.
ēmento dñe dauid Psalm̄?
et omnis mansuetudinis
eius. Sicut iurauit dño : votū

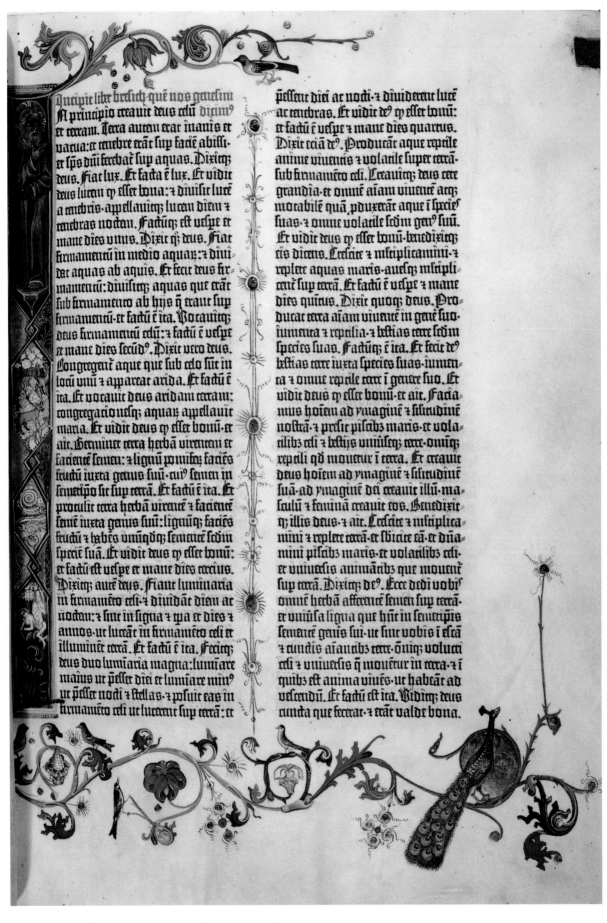

The Gutenberg Bible, ca. 1455, the first page from the Book of Genesis

THE GUTENBERG BIBLE AND EARLY PRINTING

The Library's collection of more than 5,400 incunabula (books printed before 1501) is the second largest in the United States, after the Library of Congress. It includes all fields of thought of the period and, with examples from the first and principal presses of the time, illustrates the development of the art of printing during the first half-century of its existence in Europe.

The earliest book in the collection is the Gutenberg Bible, the first substantial book printed with movable type in Europe. Printed about 1450–55, it is identified with Johann Gutenberg (1400?–68?) of Mainz, Germany, regarded as the inventor of book printing in the West. The two-volume text is in Latin, in the translation known as the Vulgate.

Only the text was printed with movable type, in characters called black-letter, or gothic. The chapter headings in red, the red and blue initials, and the large illuminated initials and marginal decorations were added by hand after the sheets were printed.

The Huntington copy is one of eleven surviving copies printed on vellum, and one of three vellum copies in America. Thirty-seven copies printed on paper also survive. Thus, a total of forty-eight copies still exist out of an estimated printing of one hundred sixty to one hundred eighty.

The bindings of the Huntington volumes—stamped calfskin covering heavy oak boards—are unusual in that they also date from the fifteenth century and are a splendid example of period craftsmanship.

About 1473–74, some twenty years after the appearance of Gutenberg's printed Bible, William Caxton, mercer, diplomat, and scholar, printed his English translation of Raoul le Fevre's *Le Recueil des Histoires de Troye*. A gathering of stories about the Trojan War, this was the first book printed in the English language. Caxton was also the first to print an edition of Chaucer's *Canterbury Tales*. In all, the Huntington has thirty-three of about a hundred works from Caxton's press.

The Huntington also holds and often displays fifteenth-century editions of Aristotle, Pliny, Euclid, and Dante, important for their influence on the course of intellectual history in the Renaissance and handsome in their craftsmanship.

TOP: *This unique engraved frontispiece of the first book printed in English, le Fevre's* Le Recueil des Histoires de Troye, *is believed to show the printer Caxton presenting the book to his patroness, Margaret, Duchess of Burgundy.*
BOTTOM: *An early printing shop in an engraving by Jan van der Straet, called Stradanus, from* Nova Reperta, *probably 1600*

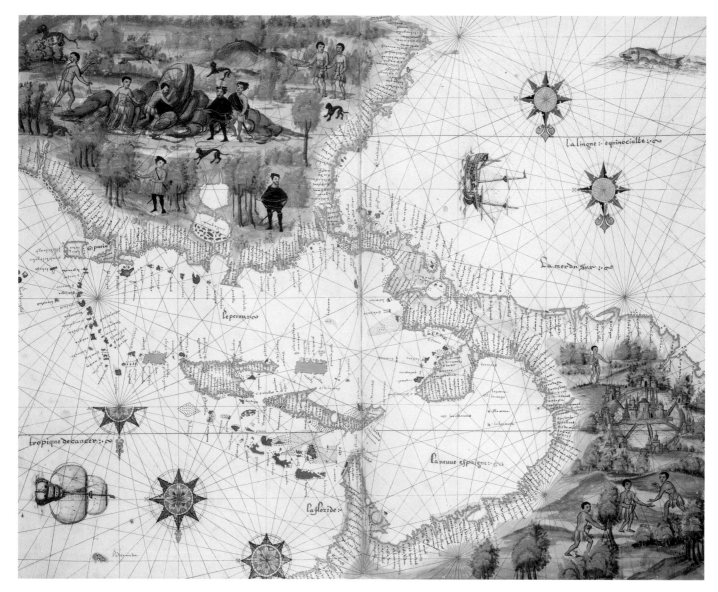

This page from the Vallard Atlas, a collection of hand-drawn maps on vellum produced in France in 1547, shows the areas under Spanish control surrounding the Caribbean Sea and the Gulf of Mexico in the seventeenth century. It includes images of indigenous peoples, animals, and vegetation as well as coastlines, coastal features, and navigational hazards, islands, towns and settlements, and an image of Tenochtitlán (Mexico City), based on the 1523 map supplied by Hernando Cortés in his letter to Charles V of Spain.

SCIENCE AND DISCOVERY

The Huntington has an important collection of fifteenth- and sixteenth-century materials on travel and exploration. Among the highlights are the King-Hamy chart of 1502, one of the first known maps to show the New World; Nicholas Vallard's magnificent illustrated atlas; and most of the early imprints of Columbus's letter describing his voyage of discovery.

The collection of works by great sixteenth- and seventeenth-century scientists represents pioneers like Italian astronomer Galileo, botanist Leonhard Fuchs, and chemist Robert Boyle, all of whom changed conventional ways of looking at the physical world. In his *Anatomical Exercises*, William Harvey gave proof of the circulation of the blood, and Isaac Newton's *Principia* defined a system of gravitational motion that was accepted for more than two centuries.

William Shakespeare and the Renaissance

The late sixteenth and seventeenth centuries mark the high point of English literary culture in the Renaissance. Dramatists of the age produced the greatest body of plays since Greek tragedy.

The best known, of course, was William Shakespeare (1564–1616). As an eminent writer, successful actor and producer, and shareholder in a theatrical company, he was a remarkable man of the theater. In addition to thirty-seven plays, he wrote a sonnet cycle, two narrative poems, and shorter verse. His works have influenced profoundly the culture of all English-speaking peoples.

The Huntington collection of early Shakespeare editions is one of the best in the world. Highlights include the 1623 first edition of his collected plays, known as the "First Folio." Entitled *Mr. William Shakespeare's Comedies, Histories, and Tragedies*, the First Folio contains thirty-six plays, eighteen of them printed for the first time; it is unquestionably the most important source of knowledge regarding Shakespeare's texts. The volume was compiled after Shakespeare's death by two of his theatrical associates.

The Library also holds other literary masterpieces, including early editions of Christopher Marlowe's *Dr. Faustus*, Edmund Spenser's *Faerie Queene*, the collected *Workes* of Ben Jonson, John Milton's *Paradise Lost*, and John Bunyan's *Pilgrim's Progress*.

More than thirty-one thousand items published in Britain before 1680 are housed in the Library, making it an important center for the study of early British literature, culture, and society.

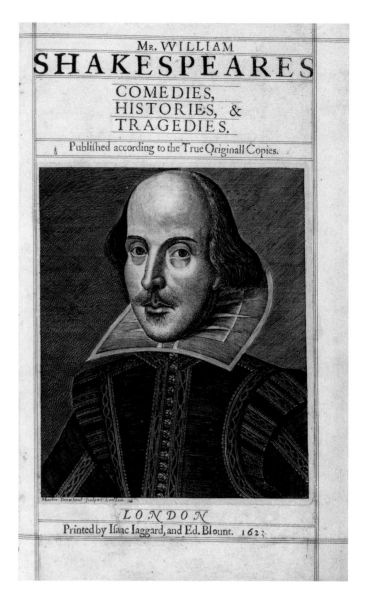

MR. WILLIAM
SHAKESPEARES
COMEDIES,
HISTORIES, &
TRAGEDIES.

Published according to the True Originall Copies.

LONDON
Printed by Isaac Iaggard, and Ed. Blount. 1623

LEFT: *"Romeo and Juliet," an eighteenth-century illustration from the Turner Shakespeare*
ABOVE: *Title page of the First Folio of 1623. This rare early edition contains the first appearance in print of most of Shakespeare's plays.*

ENGLISH LITERATURE, EIGHTEENTH TO TWENTIETH CENTURIES

The Huntington's manuscripts and first editions from this period include works by some of Britain's most celebrated poets and novelists, such as Alexander Pope, Jonathan Swift, Robert Burns, William Blake, Charlotte and Emily Brontë, William Wordsworth, John Keats, Lord Byron, Alfred Lord Tennyson, Elizabeth and Robert Browning, George Eliot, William Makepeace Thackeray, Anthony Trollope, Robert Louis Stevenson, William Butler Yeats, and James Joyce. Highlights include about 1,000 handwritten letters by Charles Dickens, notebooks containing poetry drafts, miscellaneous notes, and drawings by Percy Bysshe Shelley, a large archive for best-selling nineteenth-century novelist Jane Porter, important manuscripts and drawings by John Ruskin, and an extensive collection of material by Pre-Raphaelite figures, including Dante Gabriel Rossetti, Christina Rossetti, Holman Hunt, John Everett Millais, and Edward Burne-Jones. A large group of manuscripts and rare editions of the works of William Morris and publications from his Kelmscott Press has been augmented by the acquisition of a stunning collection relating to Morris, previously owned by collectors Sanford and Helen Berger.

Major twentieth-century collections include the archives of Kingsley Amis, Elizabeth Jane Howard, and Hilary Mantel.

Woodcut by Edward Burne-Jones for the prologue to the Canterbury Tales, *from William Morris's Kelmscott* Chaucer *(1896)*

ABOVE: *Charles Dickens in 1867 (photograph by J. and B. Gurney)*
RIGHT: *"To a Skylark" by Percy Bysshe Shelley, calligraphic and illuminated manuscript, probably by Alberto Sangorski, ca. 1910*

AMERICAN HISTORY

The collections of original documents illustrating the growth of the American republic are among the finest in existence. They are particularly strong for the Revolution, the Civil War, and the exploration and settlement of the West.

George Washington, Thomas Jefferson, and Benjamin Franklin are represented by distinguished examples of original manuscripts. Franklin's handwritten manuscript of his famous autobiography is one of the great treasures. Written between 1771 and 1790 for the benefit of his illegitimate son, William, Franklin's account of his remarkable career as statesman and scientist remains a cornerstone of American literature. George Washington's achievements can be traced through several hundred of his letters and manuscripts. These range from maps he drafted as a teenage surveyor on the Virginia frontier to letters dating from his indispensable service as commander of the Continental Army from 1775 to 1783, as president of the Constitutional Convention in 1787, and as first president of the United States from 1789 to 1797. The letters and drawings of Thomas Jefferson illustrate his varied pursuits as a revolutionary statesman, as a scientist and architect, as the president who brought about the Louisiana Purchase, as a patron of education and the arts, and as a slaveholder who agonized over America's contradictory legacy of freedom and slavery.

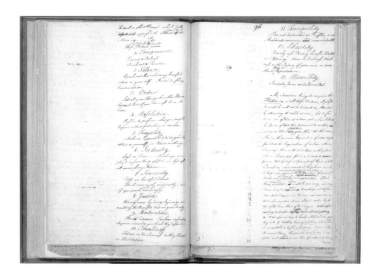

ABOVE: *A page from Benjamin Franklin's manuscript of his autobiography, written between 1771 and 1790*
BELOW LEFT: *Survey drawn by George Washington when he was 17 years old.*
BELOW RIGHT: *Thomas Jefferson's Plan for the Virginia State Capitol, drawn about 1780*

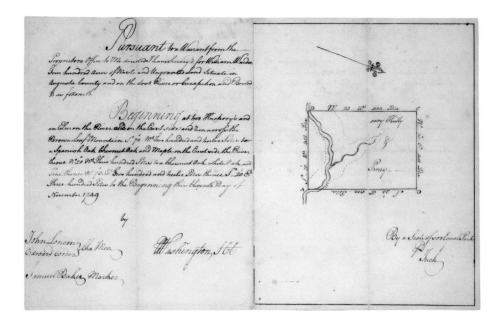

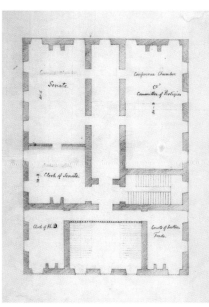

LINCOLN AND THE CIVIL WAR

The Library's splendid Civil War collections include several hundred letters of Abraham Lincoln, who, in some of the most significant examples, writes about the great issues of equality, slavery, and emancipation. In 1860, Lincoln was elected president on a platform opposing the spread of slavery into new territories. His election, followed by the secession of several slave states, ignited the American Civil War (1861–1865)—the tragic climax of decades of sectional discord. The war became the second American Revolution, a fiery trial that destroyed slavery and forged the old Union of states into a modern nation.

BELOW LEFT: *In this letter to James N. Brown in 1858, Abraham Lincoln writes, "I believe the declaration that 'all men are created equal' is the great fundamental principle upon which our free institutions rest."*
BELOW RIGHT: *Letter from Lincoln, dated April 30, 1864, authorizing General Ulysses S. Grant to conduct the campaign that was the last of the Civil War*

EXPLORATION OF THE NEW COUNTRY

In the nineteenth century, the frontier experience deeply affected American thought and feeling. Karl Bodmer, J. Goldsborough Bruff, George Catlin, and other travelers explored an unfamiliar and intensely exciting continent and pictured their findings for the world. Spurred on by visions of new opportunities available in these new lands, thousands upon thousands of emigrants journeyed to the Far West. There they encountered uncounted natural wonders and the proud native peoples who already had inhabited the region for centuries.

One of the monumental works in the effort to portray the unknown continent is John James Audubon's famous *Birds of America*. Audubon's goal was to draw every American bird from nature in its actual size. Employing Robert Havell, Jr. in London to engrave and color the plates, Audubon published the work himself. His intention was to bind each set of 100 engravings into a massive folio volume, called a double elephant folio. The resulting work contained 435 plates, comprising 4 huge volumes, each weighing nearly 46 pounds.

ABOVE: Bison-Dance of the Mandan Indians, *hand-colored engraving with aquatint by Karl Bodmer (1809–93) for Maximillian, Prince of Wied's* Travels in the Interior of North America *(1844)*
RIGHT: *Great White Heron from the double elephant folio* Birds of America *(1827–28) by John James Audubon*

CALIFORNIA HISTORY
AND LITERATURE

Mr. Huntington, who was an important figure in his own right in the history of California, began to collect materials on his adopted state late in life, creating the nucleus of what is now one of the great research collections on the subject. The Huntington's holdings range across the centuries, from the first external contacts with the indigenous peoples of California under Portolá, Serra, and Anza, to contemporary politics in a culturally diverse Southern California. The collections, comprising more than a million manuscripts, continue to grow, with particular strengths in the rancho era, the Gold Rush, land development, transportation, agriculture, ranching, legal history, and local government.

Familiar names such as Larkin, Sutter, Vallejo, O'Melveny, Patton, Banning, and Hahn share shelf space with the diaries of a Quaker missionary ministering to bracero workers in the 1940s and oral histories of early cowboys in the San Joaquin Valley. The evolving ethnic mixture of the state can be seen in the legal files of the first Chinese American immigration lawyer and the papers of the earliest African American ballet troupe in the country, while the writings of women such as Caroline Severance and Clara Burdette serve as major sources for general studies. The enormous economic growth of the state is reflected in collections such as those of the Pacific Electric/Southern Pacific and Mr. Huntington's own business papers.

ABOVE: Sutter's Fort (1849), watercolor by John Hovey
TOP RIGHT: *Faces of California, row of children on stoop at South Bunker Hill Avenue in 1957, photographed by Theodore Hall*
BOTTOM RIGHT: *This broadside published by the California Immigration Commission in 1883 typified the booster literature describing opportunities for emigrants to the Golden State.*

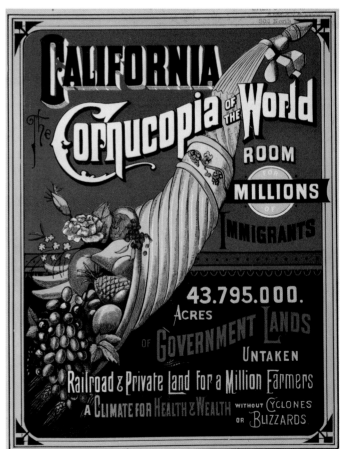

AMERICAN LITERATURE

The Library holds rare manuscripts and books for most of the important American authors of the nineteenth century. There are seven drafts plus corrected proofs for Henry David Thoreau's *Walden*, as well as other manuscripts and first editions by him and fellow New England authors Nathaniel Hawthorne, Ralph Waldo Emerson, Henry Wadsworth Longfellow, and Harriet Beecher Stowe. A superb archive for Mark Twain contains letters, handwritten drafts of *The Prince and the Pauper* and other works, and first editions of all his works.

At 50,000 items, the papers and library of Jack London comprise the largest archive in the world for the California author. Twentieth-century poets' papers include archives for Wallace Stevens, Conrad Aiken, Ann Stanford, Henri Coulette, and Robert Mezey. The Library also holds an extensive archive of scripts from the Mark Taper Forum in Los Angeles.

African Americans in the arts are documented by material for poet Langston Hughes, Los Angeles author-composer Harold Bruce Forsythe, the Los Angeles-based First Negro Classic Ballet, and playwrights Velina Hasu Houston and Sheri Bailey.

Two distinguished American poets, Robert Frost (left) and Wallace Stevens, in 1935

ABOVE: *"Boats attacking Whales,"
W. J. Linton's wood-engraved
frontispiece for Thomas Beale's*
Natural History of the Sperm
Whale *(1839). Melville praised
this illustration in his novel*
Moby Dick.
RIGHT: *Jack London, about 1900*

*Two pages from the manuscript of
Henry David Thoreau's* Walden.
*Thoreau spent six years writing this
work before its publication in 1854.*

Conservation

The Avery Conservation Center houses the Preservation Department, which is responsible for the stabilization and conservation treatment of rare books, manuscripts, photographs, and works of art on paper. The center includes conservation labs as well as an exhibitions preparation facility and digital imaging studios.

In the labs, conservators may analyze historical pigments or book bindings in order to develop treatments to refurbish rare materials. Treatments are performed with respect for the original intent of the artists and authors. Priority is given to objects that are most fragile, most valuable, or most used by scholars. In the imaging lab, copies are made of rare and unique materials, such as William Blake's watercolors, medieval and Renaissance manuscripts, and antique maps. These images serve to record and preserve the objects, and are shared with other institutions and a broad scholarly audience worldwide.

Visitors to Huntington exhibitions may sometimes wonder why the galleries seem cold or the lights dim. National conservation standards determine light, temperature, and humidity levels in the galleries to slow deterioration of the objects while they are on display. Exhibition galleries are kept at a temperature of 68 degrees and a relative humidity of 48 percent. Maintaining these standards helps to protect the collections from fading, warping, insects, and mold.

Conservator rebinds the six-hundred-year-old manuscript of Chaucer's Canterbury Tales.

Avery Conservation Center.

The main exhibition hall is open to the public,
featuring treasures of the Library.

The Charles and Nancy Munger Research Center.

THE LIBRARY IN THE TWENTY-FIRST CENTURY

The Charles & Nancy Munger Research Center, opening in 2004, will house rare materials and the conservation and photography laboratories as well as conference rooms and classrooms. The Center will provide a professional workspace for scholars and staff commensurate with the Library's collections and research programs.

THE ART COLLECTIONS

THE HUNTINGTON ART COLLECTIONS are specialized in character, focusing on eighteenth-century British and French art, and on American art ranging from the early eighteenth century to the mid-twentieth. Perhaps the best-known part of the collections is a group of British portraits from the late eighteenth century. Other objects of the same period round out the collection: French paintings, French and British sculpture, tapestries, furniture, porcelain and silver, and British drawings and watercolors. This array of distinguished furniture and decorative objects provides a congenial setting for the paintings and creates a vivid picture of the accouterments with which the aristocratic and wealthy members of late eighteenth-century society surrounded themselves.

The American art displayed in the Virginia Steele Scott Gallery consists of paintings, sculpture, and the decorative arts. The Dorothy Collins Brown wing features a full spectrum of the furniture designed by turn-of-the-twentieth-century Pasadena architects Charles and Henry Greene. The Huntington also has important collections of American drawings, prints, and photographs.

The collections are not static. The core of the British collection, including many of the most famous paintings, was assembled by Henry E. Huntington between 1908 and his death in 1927. But the collections have continued to grow by both gift and purchase, particularly in the areas of American art, drawings and watercolors, sculpture, silver, and furniture.

The main hall of the Art Gallery, with the bronze statue
Diana Huntress*, 1782, by Jean-Antoine Houdon (1741–1828)*

British Art

The British collection is remarkable for its coherence, its specialized character, and its dedication to the art of a particular time and place. In this respect it is different from the other great American art collections that were developed at the same time—in particular, those of Henry Clay Frick, P. A. B. Widener, Andrew W. Mellon, and Isabella Stewart Gardner, to name the most prominent. The Huntington offers opportunities for the study of British art of the eighteenth and early nineteenth century in a collection that for quality, variety, and depth is not surpassed outside London.

Visitors often wonder why the Huntingtons chose to concentrate their collecting as they did. The answer lies partly in Mr. Huntington's book and manuscript collections, which were focused on Anglo-American civilization and growing rapidly at the time the art collection was being formed. In addition, Mr. Huntington's personal inclination as a collector was to specialize—whether it was in early English books, desert plants, or British portraits—building a great collection around a limited area rather than spreading his attention thinly over a wide range of interests.

Many of the finest works by the most gifted English artists of the period were large formal portraits. Although most of the pictures were commissioned by the sitter or the sitters' relatives, many were also intended for public display. They made their initial appearances at the annual Royal Academy exhibition, which was then the principal artistic event of the year. A somewhat grand and rhetorical air was considered appropriate for this type of painting, and this artistic intention should be kept in mind when viewing the portraits in the Huntington collection.

Most of the people represented in these portraits knew each other. They belonged to a small, close-knit, and privileged segment of British society. Some led active and interesting lives, so we know a good deal about them. Others, although equally well placed, left almost no record of themselves.

British Paintings

The Huntington Gallery houses more than twenty full-length British portraits created in the late eighteenth and early nineteenth centuries by Joshua Reynolds, Thomas Gainsborough, George Romney, Thomas Lawrence, and other notable painters. The portraits include such famous pictures as *The Blue Boy*, *Pinkie*, and *Sarah Siddons as the Tragic Muse*.

Many of the most famous portraits are displayed in the Main Gallery, which was added to the residence in 1934 to display the larger pictures to better advantage.

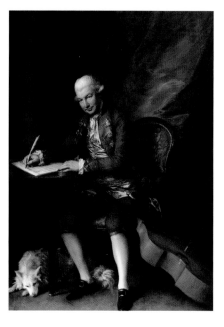

TOP: *Thomas Gainsborough,* Juliana (Howard), Baroness Petre, *1788, oil on canvas*
BOTTOM: *Thomas Gainsborough (1727–88),* Karl Friedrich Abel, *ca. 1777, oil on canvas*

Thomas Gainsborough, Jonathan Buttall:
"The Blue Boy," *1770, oil on canvas*

The most celebrated painting in this room, Gainsborough's *The Blue Boy* (ca. 1770), represents Jonathan Buttall, the son of a successful hardware merchant who was a close friend of the artist. Gainsborough dressed the boy in a costume familiar from the portraits of the great Flemish artist Anthony Van Dyck, who lived and worked in England during the early seventeenth century. Gainsborough had unbounded admiration for the work of Van Dyck and seems to have planned *The Blue Boy* as an act of homage to him.

Seven more of Gainsborough's finest works hang in the Main Gallery (in all, thirteen are on display throughout the building). It is interesting to compare the paint application in *The Blue Boy,* the earliest of these, with that in *Juliana (Howard), Baroness Petre* (1788), nearly twenty years later. As Gainsborough matured he became more assured, able to make a few brushstrokes suggest a tree, a skirt, or even a whole figure. For sheer virtuosity in the manipulation of paint, he can be considered one of the greatest artists that England has ever produced.

Thomas Lawrence's *Pinkie* (1794) faces *The Blue Boy* and is often paired with it in popular esteem, but it was painted about twenty-five years later than Gainsborough's masterpiece and had no association with the earlier painting until they both arrived at the Huntington in the 1920s. The young girl, Sarah Goodin Barrett Moulton, was born in Jamaica to a wealthy plantation family. The portrait was painted on commission for her grandmother after the girl came to England for her education. Unfortunately Sarah died a few months after the portrait was completed. Her brother, who later owned the painting, was the father of poet Elizabeth Barrett Browning.

Another portrait in the room, Joshua Reynolds's *Sarah Siddons as the Tragic Muse* (1783–84), is generally regarded as one of that artist's greatest works. It represents the then leading actress of the English stage, who specialized in tragic roles. The painting is a complex composition, filled with visual references to Michelangelo, Rembrandt, Aristotle, Ripa's *Iconologia*, and theories of the passions, all of which were understood well enough by Reynolds's contemporaries but are not likely to be familiar to present-day viewers. Yet, even without these additional levels of meaning, the painting stands in purely visual terms as one of the grandest and most dignified of British portraits.

Thomas Lawrence (1769–1830), Sarah Goodin Barrett Moulton: "Pinkie," *1794, oil on canvas*

ABOVE: *Joshua Reynolds (1723–92)*, Sarah (Kemble) Siddons as the Tragic Muse, *1783–84, oil on canvas*

TOP RIGHT: *Joshua Reynolds,* Jane Fleming, later Countess of Harrington, *1778–79, oil on canvas*

CENTER RIGHT: *George Romney (1734–1802),* The Beckford Children, *1789–91, oil on canvas*

BOTTOM RIGHT: *George Romney,* Emma Hart, later Lady Hamilton, in a Straw Hat, *before 1782–84, oil on canvas*

John Constable (1776–1837),
View on the Stour near
Dedham, *1822, oil on canvas*

Whereas portraits were the leading art form in late eighteenth-century Britain, landscape became the more popular subject for paintings in the early nineteenth century. The period was dominated by two giants, John Constable and J. M. W. Turner, who overshadowed a host of other highly gifted artists. These men were contemporary rivals, and two of the greatest artists that England ever produced.

Turner was fascinated by light and color. Partly for this reason he was drawn to the brilliant skies, marble palaces, and shimmering lagoons of Venice. His *Grand Canal: Scene—A Street in Venice* (ca. 1837) is a work from the latter part of his career. He is also represented in the collection by *Neapolitan Fisher-girls Surprised Bathing by Moonlight* (ca. 1840). This painting reveals his concern with abstract areas of light and color rather than details of things represented.

Constable's *View on the Stour near Dedham* (1822), in the Main Gallery, is considered one of the outstanding achievements not only of British but also of European landscape painting. The painting depicts a quiet stretch of country in eastern England within a couple of miles of Constable's birthplace. He painted various views of this area throughout his life, and seems never to have tired of studying the different moods created by changes in weather and atmosphere.

If Mr. and Mrs. Huntington were to walk through the Art Gallery today, they would see much that is familiar. But they would also see many items that would be new to them: the British sculpture, the silver, the sporting and genre paintings, the conversation-piece portraits, and a fair amount of British furniture.

J. M. W. Turner (1775–1851), The Grand Canal:
Scene—A Street in Venice, *ca. 1837, oil on canvas*

Louis-François Roubilliac (ca. 1695–1762), Sir Peter Warren (naval officer), marble

The Quinn Room's paneling comes from three different eighteenth-century British houses.

BRITISH SCULPTURE, FURNITURE, SILVER, AND CERAMICS

A fine representative collection of British sculpture, assembled since the 1960s, is on display throughout the Huntington Gallery. The most important piece historically, and one of the most attractive visually, is an approximately half-scale model executed in 1796 by sculptor Joseph Wilton for a commemorative monument to Archbishop Tillotson.

By and large, the British furniture acquired by the Huntingtons was for day-to-day use rather than for show. While much of it was of good and even excellent quality, comparatively few pieces reach the level of artistic interest of the British paintings or of the French decorative arts in the collections. A number of pieces of British furniture were added in 1938, when Mrs. Charles H. Quinn of Los Angeles presented her collection to the Huntington. Much of her collection, which included paintings and Chinese porcelain as well as furniture, is installed on the second floor, in a paneled room called the Quinn Room.

The silver collection, now numbering about five hundred fifty pieces, ranges in date from the fifteenth to mid-nineteenth century and covers a wider span chronologically than any other facet of British art on display in the gallery. Selections from

Silver-gilt Rosewater Ewer and Basin, made in London in 1607

the silver collection are distributed over both floors, with the most important concentrations in the North Passage and the Dining Room. Upstairs is one of the most famous pieces, John Flaxman's silver-gilt *Shield of Achilles* (1812), an outstanding example of English neoclassic art.

Most of the ceramics in the Huntington Gallery are part of an important collection of mid-eighteenth-century pieces from the Chelsea porcelain factory, famous for ornamental pieces like vases, potpourri jars, and small figures. The Chelsea porcelain is displayed in the Main and West halls on the ground floor of the gallery.

European Influences on British Art

Flemish artist Anthony Van Dyck (1599–1641) had a strong influence on English portraiture during the last half of the eighteenth century. Van Dyck had worked for Charles I in the 1630s, and his most notable work in the Huntington collection, *Anne (Killigrew) Kirke*, is of a lady of the court.

Italian painter Canaletto (1697–1768) is also represented here, with two sparkling views of Venice. Not only were his works avidly collected by Englishmen as souvenirs of their "grand tours," but Canaletto, who came to England, had a direct influence on the development of English landscape painting.

European Painting

The representation of eighteenth-century French and other European painting was greatly strengthened in 1978 when Judge and Mrs. Lucius P. Green bequeathed the Adele S. Browning Memorial Collection to the Huntington. Many of the leading French painters of the ancien régime are represented: Watteau, Pater, Lancret, Nattier, Boucher, Fragonard, Hubert Robert, Drouais, Greuze, and Prudhon. The portraits, landscapes, genre subjects, and distinctive *fêtes galantes*, in which elegant men and women disport themselves in rural surroundings, are typical of rococo art.

Dutch and Flemish seventeenth-century paintings are also represented, including the well-known *Lady with a Plume* (1636), which was produced in Rembrandt's studio. Like Rembrandt portraits of this period, it demonstrates the care taken with details of face and costume.

ABOVE: *Anthony van Dyck (1599–1805),*
Anne (Killigrew) Kirke*, ca. 1637, oil on canvas*
LEFT: *Jean-Baptiste Greuze (1725–1805),*
Young Knitter Asleep*, oil on canvas*

FRENCH DECORATIVE ART

The Huntington's collection of French furniture and decorative art, dating mostly from the eighteenth century, is one of the finest in America. Probably at no time in history has more skill and artistry gone into the design and construction of fine furniture than in France during the half century before the Revolution. All crafts concerned with the decorative arts, and especially furniture making, tapestry weaving, and porcelain manufacture, were extensively patronized by the court and aristocracy. Time and money were no object, and the quality of the finished product was always of the highest order.

Furniture (from small writing tables to chairs and large chests), tapestries, Sèvres porcelain, and decorative objects (primarily clocks and candelabra) are all represented in the collection by examples of great artistic importance. They illustrate the various styles that dominated French art from the late seventeenth until the late eighteenth century. Displays of these items can be found throughout the Huntington Gallery and the Arabella D. Huntington Memorial Art Collection.

Of particular interest is the large paneled library room on the ground floor of the Huntington Gallery. The sumptuous and elegant furnishings would have been found in a royal palace or the chateau of a wealthy aristocrat. The earliest objects are two carpets made in the late seventeenth century at the

Savonnerie factory for Louis XIV, originally part of the furnishings of the Louvre. The four splendid wall tapestries (a fifth in the suite is located in the hall outside the library) were designed by François Boucher (1703–1770). They were woven at the Beauvais factory in the mid-eighteenth century and, like the carpets, appear to have been a royal commission. The tapestries covering the chairs and settees (again from the mid-eighteenth century, but woven at the Gobelins factory) may have belonged to the mistress of Louis XV, Mme. de Pompadour.

The Library Room features late seventeenth-century Savonnerie carpets, mid–eighteenth century Beauvais wall tapestries, and library tables (detail above).

French decorative art was always a special interest for Mrs. Huntington. As a grand, final expression of affection to his wife, Mr. Huntington purchased some exquisite works in 1927 to form the basis of the Arabella D. Huntington Memorial Art Collection, which is housed in the Library building.

One room in the Memorial is devoted to French porcelain and features lavishly decorated ornamental pieces of Sèvres porcelain from the eighteenth century. Adjacent is a room of French furniture, where one can survey the evolution of French design from the middle to the end of the eighteenth century. On the walls are tapestries designed by François Boucher, part of his "Italian Village Scenes," woven on the Beauvais looms. Around the room are clocks, *torchères*, candelabras, commodes, and tables.

FRENCH SCULPTURE

The French sculpture at the Huntington comprises one of the finest collections of its kind in the country. It consists of marbles, bronzes, and terra cottas, mostly from the second half of the eighteenth century. The sculpture, like the French furniture, reflects the aristocratic elegance generally associated with that epoch. Most of the French sculpture is displayed in the Arabella D. Huntington Memorial Art Collection.

The principal sculptor represented is Jean-Antoine Houdon, one of the great artists of the eighteenth century. His *Portrait of a Lady* (1777) is one of the most important pieces in the collection. There are also objects made by (or designed by) J. B. Pigalle, Falconet, and Clodion.

RENAISSANCE BRONZES

The collection of Renaissance bronzes displayed in the small library in the Huntington Gallery is of particularly high quality. Most of the bronzes were produced in Italy or in other parts of Europe, by sculptors who had close contact with Italian art. The collection is especially rich in the work of sixteenth-century sculptor Giovanni Bologna and his followers. The majority of the bronzes were purchased by Henry Huntington en bloc from the great collection of Renaissance bronzes formed by J. Pierpont Morgan.

Although small in size (mostly between ten and twenty inches high), they exhibit the same strong sense of design and pattern found in larger sculptures. In *Nessus and Deïanira*, for example, the twist of the body of Deïanira echoes the twist of the body of the centaur, and the limbs and drapery add to the movement of the whole piece.

Renaissance bronzes display elegance, virtuosity, and meticulous craftsmanship. They are objects intended for close study.

LEFT: *Jean-Antoine Houdon,* Portrait of a Lady *(so-called Baroness de la Houze), 1777, marble*
RIGHT: *Giovanni Bologna (1529–1608),* Nessus and Deïanira, *late sixteenth century, bronze*

Roger van der Weyden (ca. 1400–1464), Madonna and Child,
oil on panel

BRITISH MINIATURE PORTRAITS

The painting of miniature portraits flourished in England from the late sixteenth to early nineteenth centuries and often commanded the talents of artists of great distinction. The Huntington collection is particularly strong in examples from the late eighteenth century, which echo the grand manner mode of presentation seen in the full-length British portraits. There is also a fine group of miniatures by masters from the seventeenth century.

Miniatures were usually given as tokens of love or affection, much as we give photographs today. They were frequently worn as jewelry by both men and women and often framed in precious stones. Normally they were painted in opaque watercolor on vellum or ivory and encased in glass. Frequently the back of the locket contained a decorative design made from the hair of the person represented.

RENAISSANCE PAINTINGS

A small group of Renaissance paintings is on display in the Arabella D. Huntington Memorial Art Collection. The paintings were collected by Arabella Huntington for her New York residence and bequeathed to her son Archer, who gave them to Henry Huntington for the Memorial Art Collection. The most important painting in the group is the *Madonna and Child* by Flemish fifteenth-century artist Roger van der Weyden— a major artist whose few identified works are considered masterpieces of Flemish Renaissance painting.

ABOVE: *Edward Norgate
(ca. 1581–1650),* Judith
Norgate, *ca. 1613, watercolor
on vellum mounted on card*
RIGHT: *Richard Cosway
(1742–1821),* George, Prince
of Wales, *1787,
watercolor on ivory*

Thomas Rowlandson, (1756–1827), A French Frigate Towing an English Man-o'-War into Port, *ca. 1790, pen and watercolor over pencil*

BRITISH DRAWINGS AND WATERCOLORS

With approximately 14,000 British drawings and watercolors, the Huntington has one of the most impressive collections outside London. While Mr. Huntington acquired a few notable groups of drawings by Blake, Rowlandson, Cosway, and the Cruikshanks, the majority of the collection has been assembled since the 1950s, when a serious program was launched to acquire British drawings as a complement to the paintings in the Huntington Gallery.

More than 500 artists are represented in the collection, covering all the important phases of British draftsmanship from the seventeenth to early twentieth centuries. The collection includes large holdings of artists such as Thomas Rowlandson, among the most popular and immediately appealing of British artists, represented here by more than five hundred items.

Many of the drawings Mr. Huntington acquired appeared in extra-illustrated books. Extra-illustrating books was a popular practice in the eighteenth and nineteenth centuries. A volume would be taken out of its binding, prints and drawings mounted and inserted between the pages, and the whole bound back together again. A book could be expanded by several volumes in the process.

WILLIAM BLAKE: REMARKABLE POET, DISTINCTIVE PAINTER

The Huntington has the most comprehensive collection in America of original watercolors, pencil drawings, manuscripts, engravings, and books by William Blake. The diversity of this collection makes it invaluable to scholars, who come from around the world to study this English poet and artist of the late eighteenth and early nineteenth centuries. His work as a painter, poet, and printmaker challenges the usual practice of separating these arts into different disciplines. Understanding one facet of Blake's work requires attention to all the others.

The richness of the Huntington's Blake holdings is best exemplified by a splendid collection of the hand-colored books of his poetry. Illuminated books, a composite art in which poetry and painting are inextricably intertwined, are considered Blake's finest and most characteristic achievements. In all, he wrote, etched, and decorated some sixteen books of his own poetry, of which the Huntington has eleven. Blake prepared few copies of each work, since they were all done by hand and the demand was small. The average number of copies of each book seems to have been about a dozen.

Blake had limited recognition as a poet and painter during his lifetime. Today, however, he is held in the highest esteem by critics, scholars, collectors, and connoisseurs. His works are among the most popular subjects in our exhibitions.

William Blake (1757–1827), The Conversion of Saul, *ca. 1800, pen and watercolor*

The Virginia Steele Scott Gallery of American Art
overlooks the Shakespeare garden.

AMERICAN ART

The Virginia Steele Scott Gallery and much of the collection it houses were gifts from the Scott Foundation in memory of art collector, patron, and philanthropist Virginia Steele Scott. Prior to the opening of the Scott Gallery in 1984, the Huntington art collection had been identified primarily with British art of the eighteenth and early nineteenth centuries. However, it had been the hope of Mr. Huntington and his advisers that the art collections expand into the American field, should the opportunity arise.

The foyer contains selections from the Mrs. John Emerson Marble Collection of Early American Silver. Beyond is a gallery devoted to twentieth-century art.

The principal space for display, straight ahead from the entrance, is a large sky-lit gallery in the form of a Greek cross. Each of the four arms of the cross displays related groups of paintings, sculptures, furniture and other decorative arts. Beyond the north arm, there is the Drawing Cabinet, a small gallery devoted to temporary exhibition of works on paper, and the Greene & Greene Room, featuring the work of Pasadena designers Charles and Henry Greene.

Though the chronological boundaries of the American art collection are expanding, the pictures it now contains were painted between the 1690s and 1940s. The collection illustrates the range of American painting for the period covered, with an emphasis on portraiture and history painting in the eighteenth century; landscape, still life, and genre painting in the nineteenth century; and social realism, regionalism, and abstraction in the twentieth century. Many of the works also show where American artists sought stylistic inspiration: frequently in England in the eighteenth and early nineteenth centuries, and increasingly in France in the late nineteenth and early twentieth centuries. In addition, the collection reveals the interest shown by American nineteenth- and early twentieth-century artists in the cultural and economic changes that transformed America from an agrarian to an industrial society and continuously pushed west the American frontier.

Most of the paintings are characteristic works by the artists concerned. John Singleton Copley's portrayal of *The Western Brothers* (1783) is a sophisticated example of the colonial artist's grand manner style. Gilbert Stuart's *George Washington* (1797) is one of several often-reproduced paintings he made of the first President of the United States. Frederic Edwin Church's *Chimborazo* (1864) is a monumental, romantic rendering of the South American landscape by a renowned member of the Hudson River School. William Michael Harnett's *After the Hunt* (1883) is a dramatic example of *trompe l'oeil* ("fool the eye") still life painting. William Merritt Chase's *Tenth Street Studio* (ca. 1880) is an inward-looking exploration of the late-nineteenth-century artist's fascination with Middle Eastern and Asian cultures. Mary Cassatt's *Breakfast in Bed* (1897) is one of the most eloquent of the painter's many impressionistic treatments of the mother-and-child theme. Walt Kuhn's *Top Man* (1931) uses strong brushstrokes and a straightforward composition to present a trapeze artist with great strength and dignity. Edward Hopper's *The Long Leg* (1935), with its simple, strong color scheme, indicates the artist's response to the growing interest in abstraction in the early twentieth century.

ABOVE: *Gilbert Stuart (1755–1828),* George Washington, *1797, oil on canvas*
RIGHT: *John Singleton Copley (1738–1815),* The Western Brothers, *1783, oil on canvas*

LEFT: *William Merritt Chase (1849–1916),* Tenth Street Studio, *ca. 1880, oil on canvas*
BELOW: *Frederic Edwin Church (1826–1900),* Chimborazo, *1864, oil on canvas*

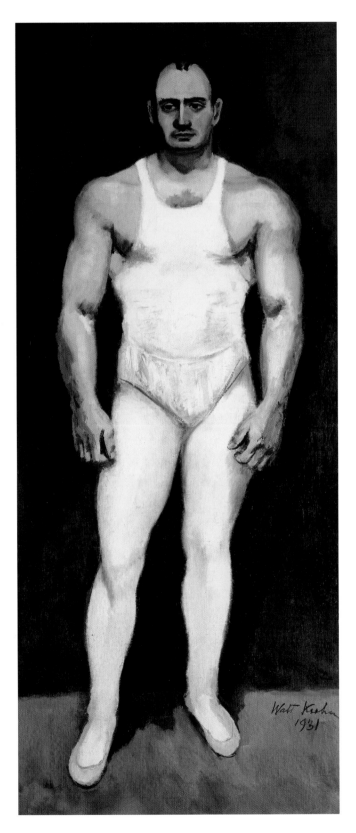

ABOVE: *William Michael Harnett (1848–1892),*
After the Hunt, *1883, oil on canvas*
RIGHT: *Walt Kuhn (1880–1949),* Top Man,
1931, oil on canvas

RIGHT: *Mary Cassatt (1845–1926),* Breakfast in Bed, *1897, oil on canvas*
BELOW: *Edward Hopper (1882–1967),* The Long Leg, *ca. 1935, oil on canvas*

Reconstruction of the dining room of the Henry M. Robinson house, 1906

Greene & Greene and the American Arts and Crafts Movement

The Dorothy Collins Brown wing of the Scott Gallery features a permanent installation of furniture and decorative arts by American architects Charles and Henry Greene who, in the early twentieth century, produced buildings and furnishings that were renowned for their design and craftsmanship.

The main hall of the gallery features the brothers' designs for both furniture and decorative objects, supplemented by paintings and decorative arts appropriate to the period. The commanding staircase in the far corner of the hall is from the Arthur A. Libby house (Pasadena, 1905; demolished in 1968), reassembled here in 1990. The adjacent gallery recreates the dining room of the Robinson house (Pasadena, 1906), reuniting furniture and a chandelier from the original commission. The Thorsen house sideboard in the main hall and the Robinson house dining room chandelier are among the most important examples of Greene & Greene furnishings.

The installation is co-curated by the Huntington and the Gamble House, University of Southern California.

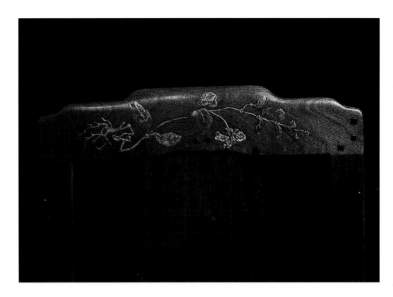

Side chair (detail), 1918-19, from the Lillian R. Thorsen house, courtesy of the Gamble House, University of Southern California

The MaryLou and George Boone Gallery

Before the Boone Gallery opened to the public in March 2000, it was known as the carriage house. Designed by Myron Hunt and Elmer Grey, the architects for the Huntington mansion and library, the original building was completed in 1911 to house Mr. Huntington's automobiles, initially both Morris cars, a limousine and a tourer, replaced later by Loziers, and later still by Locomobiles. The garden staff used Cadillacs, Oldsmobiles, and Chryslers. After Mr. Huntington's death, the building was used to store lawn mowers and other mechanical garden equipment. A generous gift from George and Mary-Lou Boone funded the transformation of the crumbling garage into a state-of-the-art exhibition gallery, providing space for the first time for major international exhibitions. Architects Levin and Associates designed the restoration of the exterior and the adaptive renovation of the interior. The building is the focal point of the Dorothy Collins Brown Garden.

The MaryLou and George Boone Gallery

THE BOTANICAL GARDENS

HUNTINGTON WAS BY NATURE a builder—of railroads, of book and art collections, and of gardens. His inclination in all of his building was to specialize, and he was satisfied with nothing less than first class. When he bought the six-hundred-acre San Marino Ranch in 1903, it was almost completely planted to citrus. Some of the original orange orchards may still be seen today, north of the Botanical Center. With the goal of creating a working estate for testing plants of potential value in the Southern California landscape, Mr. Huntington hired a twenty-six-year-old landscape gardener named William Hertrich in 1905. Over a period of two decades, they developed the basic landscape gardens and plant collections that visitors see here today. Their first efforts produced the lily ponds, followed by the palm garden and desert collection, then the North Vista, rose garden, cycad collection, and Japanese garden. By the time of Mr. Huntington's death in 1927, the estate had been reduced to two hundred acres and the orchards replaced by lawns and gardens. Improvement and development of the landscape and growth of the plant collections have continued ever since. Today, visitors can explore and enjoy twelve major garden areas, covering well over one hundred acres and containing thousands of different kinds of plants.

Mr. Huntington was always on the lookout for new plants to grow. For instance, he saved avocado seed at a gentlemen's club in Los Angeles. The seeds were planted and became an avocado grove, said to be the first commercial growth of avocados in California. From his travels he sent Hertrich seeds from melons, horse chestnuts, mountain laurel, and many other plants, all of which were destined for trial in San Marino. The botanical staff has continued his quest for exotic plants, collecting rare and useful material for research and careful introduction into the world of horticulture.

Wisteria in flower in the Japanese garden

ROSE GARDEN

The rose garden was planted in 1908 as a display garden, with several plants of each cultivar massed in symmetrical beds for color. By the 1970s the scope of the collection had grown extensively and a rose history walk was developed. Now visitors can trace the story of the rose for more than a thousand years among the two thousand cultivars on display.

The oldest cultivated Western roses, those dating back to Roman and Renaissance times, are represented by specimens in the Shakespeare garden. The beds between the Shakespeare and rose gardens, north of the rose arbor, feature tea and China roses and their descendants, first introduced into Europe from China in about 1800. On the south side of the rose arbor, in the main garden, are nineteenth-century shrub roses, descended from old European varieties. Climbing and rambling roses, from all periods and groups, grow on the arbors, arches, and pergolas.

The central portion of the rose garden contains hybrid teas, floribundas, polyanthas, and miniatures. Separate beds are planted with classic pre-1920 hybrid teas and roses from the 1920s, 1930s, and 1940s. Other beds feature roses introduced since 1950, including winners of various awards and recent introductions from abroad, most notably David Austin's Old English Roses.

SHAKESPEARE AND HERB GARDENS

The Shakespeare garden was first installed in 1957, and then redesigned in 1983 as a setting for the Virginia Steele Scott Gallery of American Art. This informal garden is the Huntington's version of an English shrubbery and perennial garden, featuring both modern and ancient plants. Among these are plants cultivated in England during Shakespeare's time and mentioned in his writings, such as pansies and violets, pinks and carnations, rosemary and other herbs, roses, pomegranates, daffodils, irises, columbines, and calendulas (marigolds). Examples of the oldest cultivated roses are found here. Of particular historical interest are the White Rose of York and the Red Rose of Lancaster, which originated before the Christian era and were emblems of opposing factions during the fifteenth-century Wars of the Roses.

The attractive formal herb garden has plantings arranged according to the uses made of the herbs: medicines; teas; liqueurs; cooking, salads, and confections; cosmetics, perfumes, and soaps; potpourris and sachets; insect repellents; and dyes.

The half-acre formal herb garden

The Shakespeare garden is a showcase of flowering perennials.

*In the Baja California
bed, creeping devil
(RIGHT) grows spiny
stem segments that
spread across the ground.
The pincushion cacti
(BELOW), one of the
finest collections to be
seen anywhere, are more
contained.*

DESERT GARDEN

For many visitors, the most unusual aspect of the Botanical Gardens is the ten-acre desert garden. More than four thousand species of desert plants present a startling display of odd forms and shapes. The area is not intended to represent a desert—it is a landscaped garden with specimens planted where they will grow best. Many beds reflect floristic relationships, with plants grouped by geographic area.

The collection includes many species of xerophytes, plants that are adapted to arid environments. Though they come from dry regions around the world, many xerophytes resemble one another, having evolved similar strategies for survival. Some store water in their stems or leaves in order to survive in dry climates. Many protect themselves from herbivores with sharp spines or thorns, and some have waxy or wooly coverings that reflect the sun, decreasing the impact of solar heat and evaporation. These adaptations sometimes result in strange or even grotesquely shaped plants: the ribbed and spiny barrel cactus; the columnar organ-pipe cactus; the mammillarias, cushion-like plants ranging in diameter from a few inches to three feet; and the opuntias, like the flat-jointed prickly pear, or those with cylindrical joints, known as cholla.

LEFT: *Colorful aloes in bloom*
BELOW LEFT: *Variegated* Agave americana
BELOW RIGHT: *Plume-like flower stalk of* Nolina matapensis, *rarely seen in cultivation, overlooks a crowd of barrel cactus.*

TOP: *Conical yellow flowers of aeonium droop under their own weight. Beyond is the dazzling* Lampranthas *'Rose Carpet.'*
BOTTOM: *Hundreds of pink blossoms—popular with bees and honey-eating birds—cover the spires of 'Tower of Jewels.'*

The conservatory houses rare cacti and succulents too tender to survive outdoors.

The welwitschia only has two leaves.

The largest cactus on the grounds is *Cereus. Cereus xanthocarpus*, for example, weighs some fifteen tons. *Cereus huntingtonianus*, a massive specimen with crimson buds and outside petals, was first described from this garden and named for Mr. Huntington.

Throughout the garden are many kinds of crassulas, including the echeverias, native to Mexico, which vary from tiny rosettes to large, cabbage-leaved specimens more than a foot tall, and aeoniums, an Old World group from the Canary Islands.

At the upper end of the garden is a conservatory housing succulents that require controlled conditions. Some of the plants demonstrate mimicry, camouflaging themselves against the stones of their native habitats. Others produce clear tissue in their leaves, which allows sunlight to strike photosynthetic cells deep inside. Still others, such as the American cacti and certain African euphorbias, demonstrate the convergent evolution of like forms in very different plant groups.

Among such plants, the most notable is a collection of *Lithops* species, South African members of the ice plant family,

famed for its rock-like leaves. In nature, each species grows on ground of the same color. Red-leaved *Lithops aucampiae* grows almost completely buried in reddish soil, whereas the whitish *Lithops gracilidelineata* thrives among white quartz pebbles. Tiny *Titanopsis calcarea*, of the same family, looks so much like the surface of the limestone rocks on which it grows that it was discovered accidentally by an African botanist who leaned against a rock and crushed a plant with his hand.

One great botanical curiosity is *Welwitschia mirabilis*. The species name *mirabilis* means "marvelous," an adjective that is well deserved. Scattered along the rainless desert of coastal Namibia and Angola, these plants lie sprawled like so many stranded sea monsters. During a long lifetime, *Welwitschia* produces only two leaves that lengthen continually from their base. When protected, the leaves may grow to a length of ten feet before becoming frayed and torn at their tips by desert winds. Though *Welwitschia* looks nothing like a pine or cycad, it bears cones as those ancient plants do and may have existed long before flowering plants evolved.

Heart of Flame bromeliad

A dense mat of echeveria rosettes

This yucca has needle-sharp leaves.

Lithops match their ground color.

JAPANESE GARDEN

West of the rose garden is the Japanese garden, distinguished by its curving walks, flowing water, and small, still ponds; artistically placed stones and statuary; and painstakingly pruned and trained plants. There are no broad vistas or symmetrical plantings, as you would find in formal gardens. Some visitors find that the informal design, abundant green foliage, simple forms, and restrained scale in this garden create a sense of natural order and tranquility.

When Mr. Huntington acquired the ranch, the present Japanese garden was a rugged gorge surrounded by a tangle of trees, wild grapevines, and poison oak. In 1911 major construction was undertaken to build terraces, ponds, and paths, and install a Japanese tea garden purchased intact at its Pasadena site. The purchase included twenty-five truckloads of mature plants and a complete house that was sawed apart, transported, and reassembled at its current location.

Elements of this five-room house came originally from Japan. Two of the rooms have alcoves, called *tokonomas*, which each feature a seasonal scroll and a traditional Japanese flower arrangement, or *ikebana*, created in the style of the Ikenobo school, the oldest school of Japanese flower arranging. Members of the San Marino League have created these flower arrangements and helped with restoring and maintaining the garden since 1957.

Other notable structures in the garden include the temple gong tower and the moon bridge. The gong is Buddhist, and its inscription states that it was cast in 1766 for Kongo Buji Temple on Mt. Koya.

The moon bridge was constructed specifically for the garden. Highly arched bridges like this one were a feature of Chinese garden architecture, which was then adopted by Japanese craftsmen in the thirteenth century. They are known as moon bridges because the arch and its reflection in the water below form a full moon shape. Viewing the moon and its reflection in ponds and lakes was a traditional activity of cultural life. Dominating the scene around the bridge is a weeping willow tree, a native of China. Near the other end are unusually large specimens of *Cycas revoluta* (cycads).

The garden features many other plants commonly found in a Japanese garden, including Japanese maples, Japanese red and black pines, azaleas, and camellias. Paths leading north from the Japanese house pass through a shelter of live oaks, pines, cherry trees, and camphor en route to the Chinese garden. The sloping canyon boasts hundreds of camellia cultivars.

A juniper serpentines across a highly textured stone bridge in a hidden corner of the Japanese garden.

The Japanese house, accented by informal plantings of camellias, azaleas, wisteria, and flowering fruit trees, overlooks the moon bridge and pond.

TOP LEFT: *Temple gong tower has authentic tile roof*
TOP RIGHT: *Stone pagoda is an example of the many ornaments in the garden*
ABOVE: *The interior of the Japanese house*

To the south, zigzag bridges pass over a "dry streambed" in which rocks and pebbles simulate water and lead to the Zen and bonsai courts. The Zen court features a dry, raked landscape known as a *karesansui* in Japanese. This type of garden evolved in temple compounds in the context of Zen Buddhism. A slate walk passes through the center of the court, with a grove of ginkgo trees on one side and the *karesansui* on the other. An open expanse of gravel, raked in a pattern suggestive of flowing water, the *karesansui* is broken here and there by rocks, ending in a line of trees and shrubs suggesting a far bank. This garden was inspired by the main garden at Daitokuji, near Kyoto, created in the mid-sixteenth century.

Courtyards beyond the stucco wall were developed to display bonsai, dwarf trees that are trained in the Japanese style. Bonsai is a Japanese art form now relatively well known in the West. The aim is to produce trees in miniature, whether a whole grove or a single gnarled, weather-twisted patriarch. Originating as a display of seven specimens, the bonsai courts today house one of the Golden State Bonsai Federation collections and benefit from the support of bonsai clubs and artists from all over California.

Mixed in with the bonsai are handsome water-washed and weathered stones, called *suiseki*, another Japanese art form. A *suiseki* is a water-sculpted stone, carefully chosen to represent a natural phenomenon such as a distant mountain, a cascade, or an island in the sea. In North America the art has expanded to include wind-eroded specimens found in the desert.

ABOVE: *The raked gravel garden (*karesansui*)*
RIGHT: *Opposite the* karesansui *is a grove of ginkgos, also known as maidenhair trees. They turn a bright yellow in the fall.*

CYCADS

The Huntington's cycad collection is one of the oldest in the United States. Examples can be seen in the jungle, Australian, Japanese, desert, and palm gardens, as well as in plantings surrounding the Art Gallery.

The collection was started in 1910 with a few plants collected in Mexico. In 1913 some exceptional specimens arrived from Japan, including plants said to be between 300 and 400 years old. Among these may have been the large clumps of *Cycas revoluta* near the Huntington Art Gallery and in the Japanese garden.

These "living fossils" are relics of an ancient and extensive cycad flora that thrived alongside the dinosaurs during the early Mesozoic era. Today most cycads are found in the warmer regions of Australia, Asia, Africa, and North and South America. Although palmlike in appearance, cycads are in fact more closely related to pines, producing seed in cones rather than flowers.

Cycad cones sometimes resemble pineapples, like the ones above, or pine cones, like the ones at left. Male and female cones are produced on separate plants.

TOP LEFT:
Eucalyptus
macrocarpa *has the*
largest flowers
of all eucalyptus.
TOP RIGHT:
The red, bell-shaped
flowers of the flame
tree stand out against
the less showy
eucalyptus trees in the
Australian garden.
RIGHT:
The brilliant flowers
of the kangaroo paw
'Pink Joey'

AUSTRALIAN GARDEN

With a landmass roughly the size of the United States, Australia is home to more than 25,000 species of plants, most of them found nowhere else. The five-acre Australian garden was created to display trees and shrubs that represent this diversity of flora. There are plants in flower here throughout the year, beginning in January with the blooming of the acacias and continuing on through the flowering of the kangaroo paws, melaleucas, wax flowers, and blue hibiscus, bottlebrushes, eucalyptus, and brachychitons.

Some of the smaller, shrub-like eucalypts are extremely colorful, with red, pink, and bright yellow flowers, while varieties of the well-known bottlebrush become flaming masses of scarlet. One of the most profusely flowering shrubs is the mint bush (*Prostanthera*), with aromatic leaves and masses of purple blossoms.

The garden also features herbaceous plants, such as the unusual kangaroo paws, named for the shape of their intriguing pink, red, green, and yellow flowers.

PALM GARDEN

Palms were of particular interest to Mr. Huntington, especially because of their suitability for the Southern California landscape. Most palms are native to wet, tropical regions of the world, but at least 300 species can survive the low rainfall and cool winters of Southern California. Most of these are represented in the palm garden and adjacent jungle garden. Of special note are huge clumps of the European fan palm, a massive multi-trunk specimen of the date palm, and a great diversity of American braheas. In one afternoon, visitors can learn to identify all of the common palms in the California landscape.

ABOVE: *This blue hesper palm from Baja California has silvery-blue fronds and a massive trunk.*
LEFT: *More than 200 species of palms thrive in the Huntington's temperate climate.*

SUBTROPICAL AND JUNGLE GARDENS

To visitors from the colder parts of the United States, California may seem tropical, and many of the plants grown at the Huntington are so exotic as to appear tropical. In fact, California and four other regions at the same latitude on the western coasts of continents have what is termed a Mediterranean climate, with hot, dry summers and mild, comparatively wet winters. This climate supports open, chaparral-type vegetation, and gardeners here cultivate plants from many other areas of the world, particularly the warmer Mediterranean and subtropical zones. Although there are plants from these areas throughout the gardens, the subtropical garden features them extensively. This garden also includes plants from southwestern Australia, the Cape Provinces of South Africa, the coast of Chile, and the Mediterranean basin.

Covering a four-acre slope south of the rose garden and the Art Gallery, the garden is south-facing, and consequently nearly frost-free. Until the twentieth century, it was covered with oaks and grasses, and coast live oaks are still to be seen here. One of the paths was part of the road that was used by the Huntingtons and their neighbors, the Pattons, when they visited one another.

Prominent in the plantings are various species of *Tabebuia*, spectacular flowering trees, and the jacaranda, a Brazilian tree with a dazzling show of blue flowers in late spring. Yellow-flowering cassias are well represented, both as shrubs and large trees. Along one path is *Bauhinia blakeana*, the most resplendent of the orchid trees, with deep mauve flowers. Only one plant of this tree was ever discovered in the wild, in the hills above Hong Kong, and all existing cultivated specimens are its descendants.

The jungle garden, along the same south-facing slope, features plants that can survive cool nights and occasional frosts, creating the ambience of a tropical forest. These include gingers, ferns, palms, bamboos, and many members of the arum family.

TOP: *Lily pond in the jungle garden with bird of paradise, calla lilies, bamboo, and papyrus*
ABOVE: *Lotus flowers in the lower lily ponds*
RIGHT: *Yellow flowering tabebuia is a spring showstopper in the subtropical garden.*

Waterfall in the jungle garden, with flowering bromeliads

A baroque fountain adorns the far end of the North Vista.

NORTH VISTA AND ART GALLERY GARDEN

The North Vista's combination of greenery, flowering shrubs, and long lines of sculpture is the most formal garden space at the Huntington. The stone statues lining the lawn were made in the seventeenth century for a European garden and purchased by Mr. Huntington at an auction in 1922. The large stone fountain at the far end of the North Vista was imported from Italy and is a handsome example of the early baroque style in sculpture.

Around the Huntington Art Gallery are informal and exotic plantings that represent Mr. and Mrs. Huntington's favorites, from cycads and palms to cymbidium orchids and ferns. The collection of cycads in the rockery is particularly mature; some of these large specimens are more than two hundred years old. On the balustrade of the south terrace are two species of staghorn ferns (*Platycerium*) from Australia and Indonesia. In the wild, these ferns cling to tree branches and cliffs.

One of the more unusual trees in this garden is the white floss silk tree (*Chorisia insignis*) from Peru. It has a thorny, swollen trunk for storing water. In the autumn and winter its bare branches are covered with white flowers; in the spring it bears large seed pods that burst open with a shower of whitish, kapok-like fibers.

The Camellia Collection

The garden surrounding the North Vista contains cultivars of the three most commonly grown species of camellias (*Camellia sasanqua*, *Camellia japonica*, and *Camellia reticulata*) and extensive companion plantings of azaleas that bloom from October to early spring. More than fifty additional camellia species, including *Camellia sinensis* (the source of tea) and more than fourteen hundred cultivars are represented in the area from the North Vista to the developing Chinese garden, North Canyon, and Japanese garden.

TOP LEFT: Camellia japonicas *are the backdrop for this statue on the North Vista.*
TOP RIGHT: Camellia sinensis, *the tea plant*
ABOVE, LEFT TO RIGHT: C. sasanqua *'Snowfall';* C. japonica *'Jack McCaskill';* C. reticulata *'Purple Gown'*

RIGHT: Cupid Blindfolding Youth *(detail, near right) and the* Rape of Persephone *are two of the statues near the North Vista.*
BELOW: Flora *by Antoine Coysevox (1640–1720)*

GARDEN SCULPTURE

One of the most delightful and distinctive features of the Huntington gardens is the sculpture. Most of it dates from the late seventeenth and early eighteenth centuries and was made in northern Italy, southern Germany, and France.

Most garden sculpture, including that at the Huntington, was intended to be part of a larger ensemble. The themes are often vague and the execution sketchy, but the pieces are frequently charming and entertaining. Amatory episodes usually play a prominent role. Near the entrance to the North Vista, for instance, Cupid is blindfolding Youth; in the Rose Garden, Love is the captive of Youth; and no less a person than Louis XV is shown guided by Love in the tempietto on the south lawn below the Art Gallery.

Of the many statues lining either side of the North Vista, twenty were made in the seventeenth century in Italy and were originally located in a villa near Padua. Some figures are easy to identify, such as Perseus with the head of Medusa, or Athena in her helmet and armor; others are more difficult to place. The formal vista is dominated by a grand seventeenth-century Idrian fountain at the north end.

Probably the most charming of the garden sculptures are the four large terra cottas on the loggia of the Art Gallery. Each is associated with a prominent French sculptor of the eighteenth century.

BOTANICAL CENTER

The public is welcome to visit the children's garden, teaching greenhouse, labs, workshops, classrooms, and displays for the home gardener to take advantage of opportunities to study and appreciate plants. The spectacular Rose Hills Foundation Conservatory for Botanical Science, in particular, offers many opportunities for children and adults to touch and examine plants. The center also houses special research and training facilities to support work by visiting scientists and provide professional development for teachers at many levels.

CHINESE GARDEN

The first phase of a twelve-acre Chinese garden is scheduled to open to visitors in 2006. It will feature a central pond surrounded by a large collection of Asian plants. Located in the center of the grounds and framed by an existing woodland, the garden will include a teahouse, pavilions, bridges, and other natural and architectural features.

RIGHT: *The first phase of the Chinese garden*
BELOW: *The Rose Hills Foundation Conservatory for Botanical Science*

Research and Education

Huntington was aware that his collections aroused both scholarly and public interest. He allowed scholars access to the libraries he acquired, at times even inviting them into his home. Similarly, because of the growing public curiosity triggered by newspaper coverage of his purchases, he allowed his staff to mount small exhibitions and open the grounds to visitors on a limited basis.

Prior to his death, he appointed the first Director of Research, Max Farrand, a distinguished historian, to manage his legacy. Farrand in turn immediately brought the most famous American historian of that time, Frederick Jackson Turner, to the library as the first resident scholar. Farrand also opened the institution to the public and provided them with such amenities as parking spaces and restrooms. Since that time, millions of people have enjoyed the beauty of the gardens, the specialized art collection, and the Library's extraordinary holdings of rare books and manuscripts.

Although much has changed over the years, the Huntington is still engaged in the same mission, although the collections are much larger as a result of an active acquisition policy. Scholars from around the world are still drawn to the collections to research issues that are in the forefront of scholarship today—ranging from women's studies, to exploration and discovery of the Americas, to the ongoing speculation over the identity of Shakespeare. The results of research are shared through seminars, conferences, lectures, and publications.

Weekly seminars feature speakers from around the world exchanging views with professors from local colleges and universities. Conferences on topics of current interest are also catalysts that advance learning in the humanities. A dynamic lecture program connects leading historians and literary scholars with a community audience.

Ahmanson Reading Room

Huntington Library Quarterly

Volume 59   Number 4

The Huntington Library Press has been publishing books on literature, art, history, and gardens since 1920, and since 1937, a scholarly journal.

Over the years, many distinguished scholars have participated in these seminars and conferences while pursuing their investigations at the Huntington. Their resulting scholarship has won many prizes, including the Pulitzer.

Scholarship is also shared through an active publication program. The Huntington published its first books in 1920, facsimiles of two sixteenth-century plays, *Fulgens and Lucrece* and *Enough is as Good as a Feast*. Since then a steady flow of editions, facsimiles, monographs, and catalogs have drawn on Huntington collections to produce many notable works, including a series of classics on the history of the American West, a facsimile of a fifteenth-century illuminated manuscript of Chaucer's *Canterbury Tales*, and an edition of Robert Louis Stevenson's *Kidnapped* based on the Library's manuscript.

The education program has experienced a huge expansion in the decades since those first small exhibits in the library reading room. In recent years, the Huntington has mounted comprehensive exhibits on Abraham Lincoln, George Washington, the California Gold Rush, British paintings, and the art and science of astronomy, among other subjects. Some of these exhibits have been reformatted for presentation in libraries around the country; others can be viewed on the Huntington's web site, www.huntington.org.

In addition to exhibitions, the Huntington offers an extraordinary array of learning experiences for students of all ages, from toddlers to senior citizens, including teachers and other professionals.

A typical day begins with local students participating in programs that enrich their schoolwork in art, botany, and the humanities. In the afternoon, docents lead adult tours through the gardens and answer visitors' questions in the Library Exhibition Hall. In one corner of the gardens, families participate in a hands-on workshop while in another, children as young as three cluster around a discovery cart, where they work on activities related to nature and the gardens. Meanwhile, in the laboratories of the Botanical Center, teachers are studying plants and working on botany experiments. At the same time, new docents are being trained to teach in the art galleries. In the Library, interns from Latin America are receiving advanced training in conservation techniques. Nearby, in a seminar room, the Los Angeles study group meets to consider a paper by a graduate student from a local university. In another seminar room, the staff teaches paleography (early handwriting) to graduate students. In the evening, Friends' Hall fills with academics and other adults interested in lifelong learning to hear a lecture on the history of the American West.

TOP LEFT: *Each year thousands of students attend docent-led classes. This one is called "Reading Plants."* BOTTOM LEFT: *A group tour of the Japanese garden* TOP RIGHT: *Weeklong summer programs for youngsters include time to study plants up close in the botanical lab.* BOTTOM RIGHT: *Ducks in the lily ponds are used to visitors.*

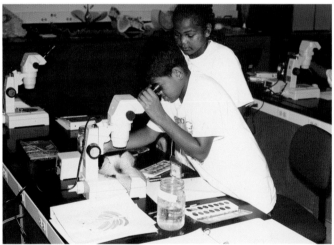

A Calendar of Color

January
ART GALLERY: Kaffirboom Coral Tree,
    Pink Ball Dombeya
AUSTRALIAN: Bailey Acacia
DESERT: Aloes
JAPANESE: Japanese Flowering Apricot
NORTH VISTA: Japonica and Sasanqua
    Camellias
ROSE GARDEN: Asiatic Magnolias
SHAKESPEARE: Iceland Poppies

February
ART GALLERY: Pink Ball Dombeya
AUSTRALIAN: Bailey Acacia
CAMELLIA GARDENS: Reticulata and
    Japonica Camellias
DESERT: Aloes, Euphorbias,
    Mesembryanthemums
JAPANESE: Japanese Flowering Apricot,
    Azaleas, Flowering Peaches,
    Formosan Cherry, Magnolias,
    Michelia doltsopa
NORTH VISTA: Azaleas, Reticulata and
    Japonica Camellias
ROSE GARDEN: Magnolias
SHAKESPEARE: Flowering Peaches,
    Iceland Poppies, Narcissus, Cherry,
    Magnolias, Michelia doltsopa

March
AUSTRALIAN: Australian Shrubs
CAMELLIA GARDENS: Reticulata and
    Japonica Camellias
DESERT: Desert Cassias, Euphorbias,
    Mesembryanthemums
HERB: Lady Banks Roses
JAPANESE: Flowering Cherries, Azaleas,
    Flowering Peaches, Magnolias,
    Wisteria, Reticulata Camellias
NORTH VISTA: Azaleas, Reticulata and
    Japonica Camellias

PARKING LOT: Snowball Bush
ROSE GARDEN: Wisteria, Lady Banks Roses
SHAKESPEARE: Ranunculus, Narcissus
SUBTROPICAL: Golden Trumpet Tree,
    Hong Kong Orchid Tree, Lady
    Banks Roses, Skyrocket Flower,
    S. African bulbs

APRIL
ART GALLERY: Easter Lily Vine
AUSTRALIAN: Australian Mint Bush
DESERT: Puyas
HERB: Roses
JAPANESE: California Native Iris,
    Wisteria
LIBRARY AREA: Bidwill's Coral Tree,
    Mexican Coral Tree
ROSE GARDEN: Roses, Wisteria, Iris,
    Chinese Fringe Tree
SHAKESPEARE: Columbines, Dianthus,
    Iris, Roses, Snowball Bush
SUBTROPICAL: Golden Trumpet Tree,
    Skyrocket Flower

MAY
ART GALLERY: Bougainvillea, Easter
    Lily Vine
AUSTRALIAN: Australian Bottlebrushes
DESERT: Cacti, Puyas
HERB: Roses, Herbs
ROSE GARDEN: Roses, Iris, Lavender
    Trumpet Vine, Perennial Border
SHAKESPEARE: Columbines,
    Delphiniums, Iris, Roses
SUBTROPICAL: Cassias, Jacaranda

JUNE
AUSTRALIAN: Australian Bottlebrushes,
    Eucalyptus, Kangaroo Paws
DESERT: Cacti, Yuccas
HERB: Herbs

JAPANESE: Lacebark Bottle Trees,
    Hydrangeas
NORTH VISTA: Hydrangeas
PARKING LOT: Daylilies, Leonotus,
    Oleanders
ROSE GARDEN: Roses, Agapanthus,
    Delavay Magnolia, Perennial Border
SUBTROPICAL: Jacaranda

JULY
ART GALLERY: Moreton Bay Chestnut
AUSTRALIAN: Eucalyptus, Kangaroo Paws
DESERT: Yuccas
HERB: Herbs
JAPANESE: Lacebark Bottle Trees
LILY PONDS: Water Lilies, Lotus
NORTH VISTA: Hydrangeas
PARKING LOT: Leonotus
ROSE GARDEN: Roses
SHAKESPEARE: Daylilies
SUBTROPICAL: Cape Chestnut, Golden
    Medallion Cassia

AUGUST
ART GALLERY: Moreton Bay Chestnut
AUSTRALIAN: Eucalyptus, Kangaroo Paws
HERB: Crepe Myrtles
LILY PONDS: Water Lilies
ROSE GARDEN: Roses
SHAKESPEARE: Summer Annuals
SUBTROPICAL: Giant Daisies, Salvias

SEPTEMBER
ART GALLERY: Floss Silk Trees
AUSTRALIAN: Australian Shrubs and Trees
DESERT: Floss Silk Trees
LIBRARY AREA: Bidwill's Coral Tree
LILY PONDS: Chinese Lotus
ROSE GARDEN: Delavay Magnolia
SHAKESPEARE: Summer Annuals
SUBTROPICAL: Cassias, Floss Silk Trees

OCTOBER
ART GALLERY: Floss Silk Trees, Gingers
AUSTRALIAN: Australian Shrubs and Trees
DESERT: Floss Silk Trees
HERB: Saffron Crocus
JAPANESE: Japanese Anemones, Gingers,
    Sweet Olive
LIBRARY AREA: Bidwill's Coral Tree
ROSE GARDEN: Roses
SHAKESPEARE: Pansies, Saffron Crocus
SUBTROPICAL: Cassias, Floss Silk Trees,
    Gingers

NOVEMBER
ART GALLERY: Floss Silk Trees,
    Cup-of-Milk Vine
AUSTRALIAN: Mallee Eucalyptus
CAMELLIA: Sasanqua Camellias
DESERT: Floss Silk Trees
JAPANESE: Fall Foliage Color, Sweet
    Olive
NORTH VISTA: Himalayan Cherry,
    Sasanqua Camellias
ROSE GARDEN: Roses
SUBTROPICAL: Floss Silk Trees

DECEMBER
ART GALLERY: Floss Silk Trees, Poinsettias
CAMELLIA: Sasanqua Camellias
DESERT: Floss Silk Trees, Aloes, Crassulas
JAPANESE: Early Magnolias
NORTH VISTA: Himalayan Cherry,
    Sasanqua Camellias
ROSE GARDEN: Roses
SHAKESPEARE: Iceland Poppies
SUBTROPICAL: Floss Silk Trees

OVERLEAF: *The North Vista.*

Index

Illustration pages are indicated by bold type.